How Many Ani

by Anne Diorio

Look!

I see 1 koala.

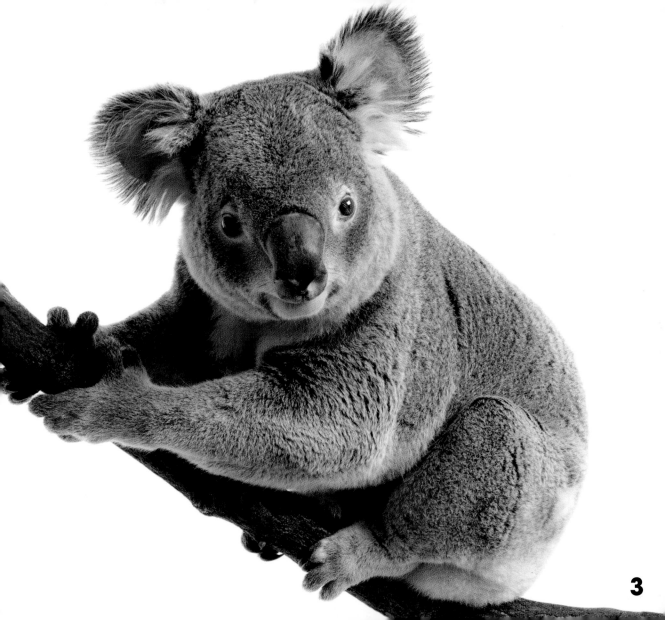

Look!

I see 2 lions.

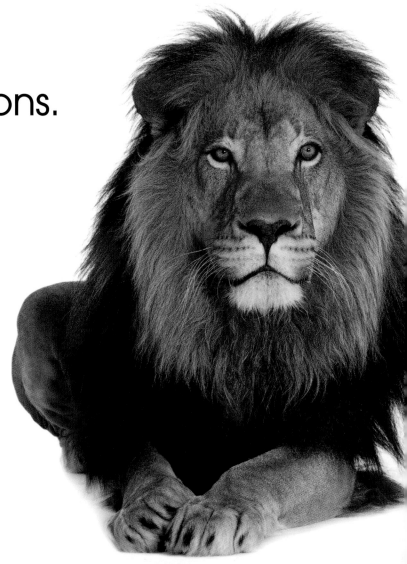

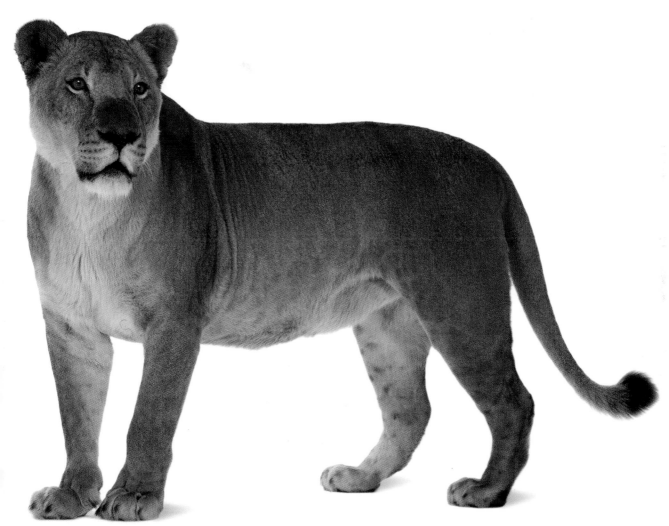

Look!

I see 3 parrots.

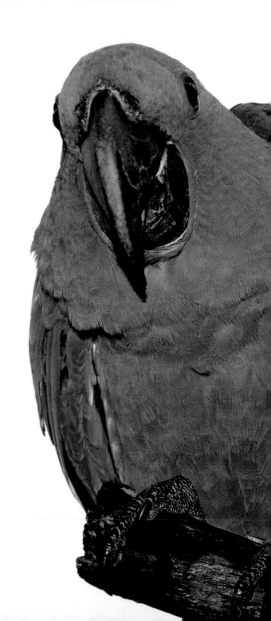

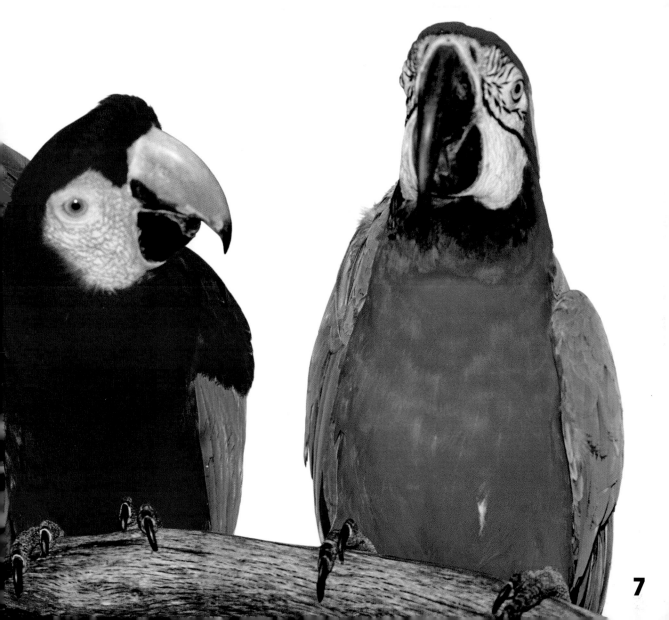

Look!

I see 4 flamingos.

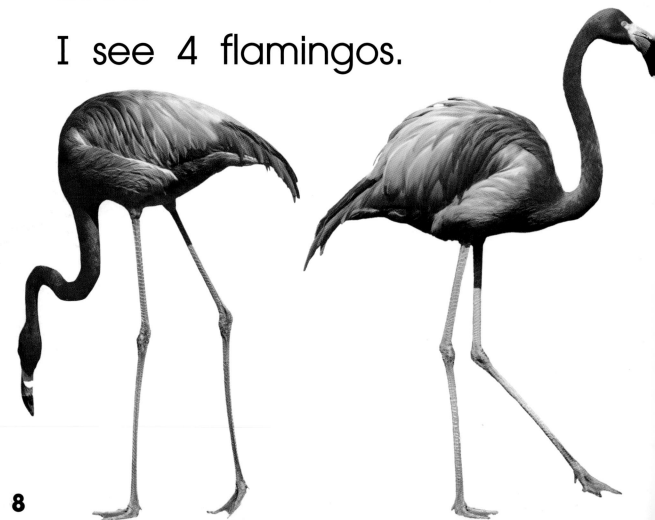

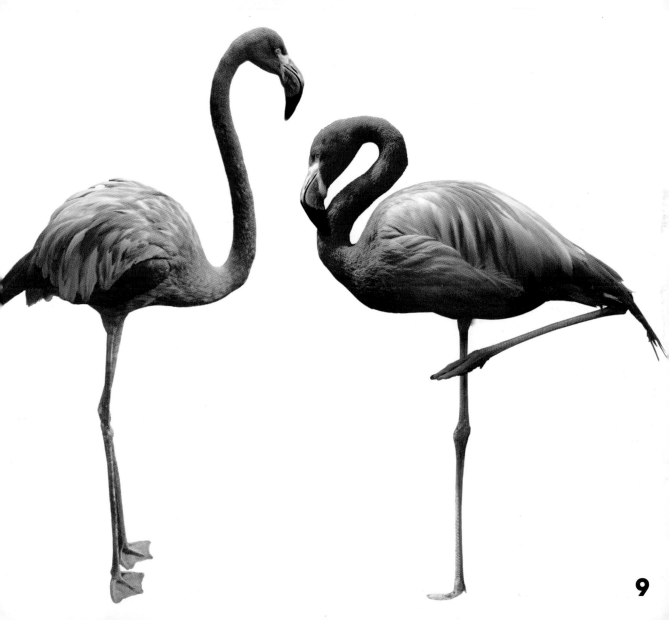

Look!

I see 5 seals.

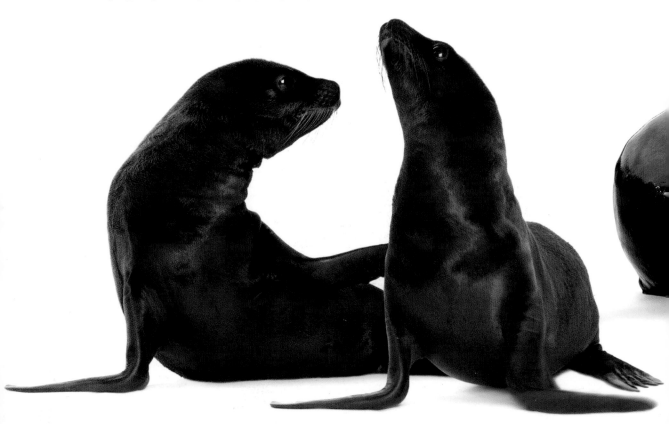

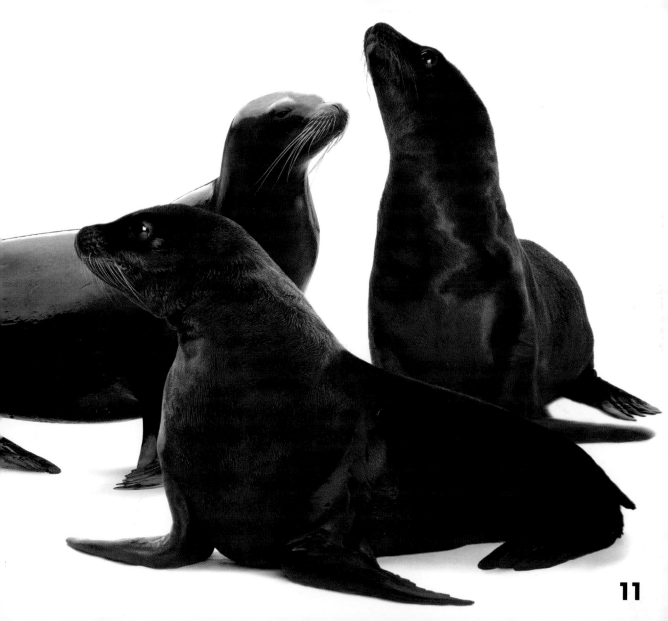

Look!

I see 6 monkeys.

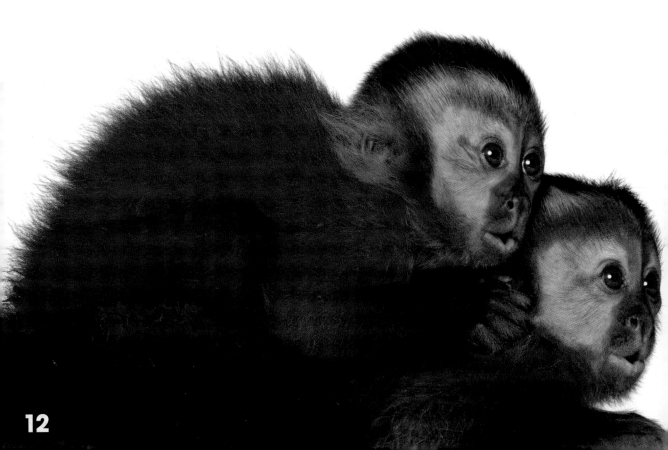

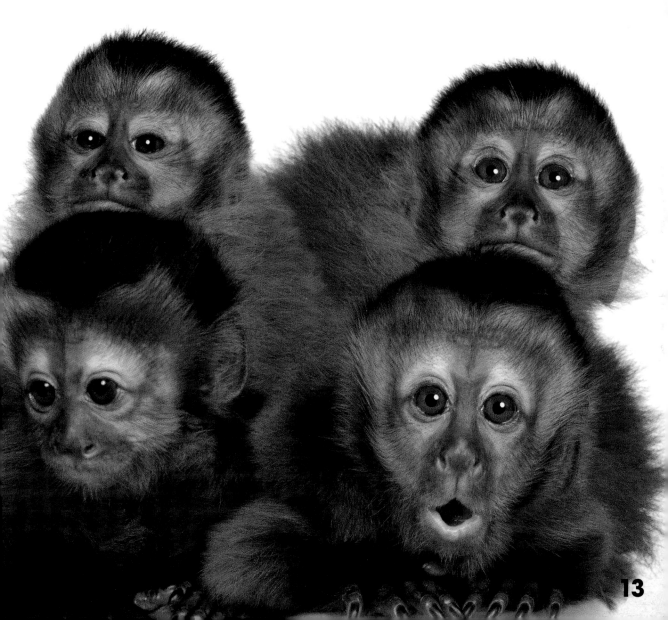

Look!

I see 7 kangaroos.

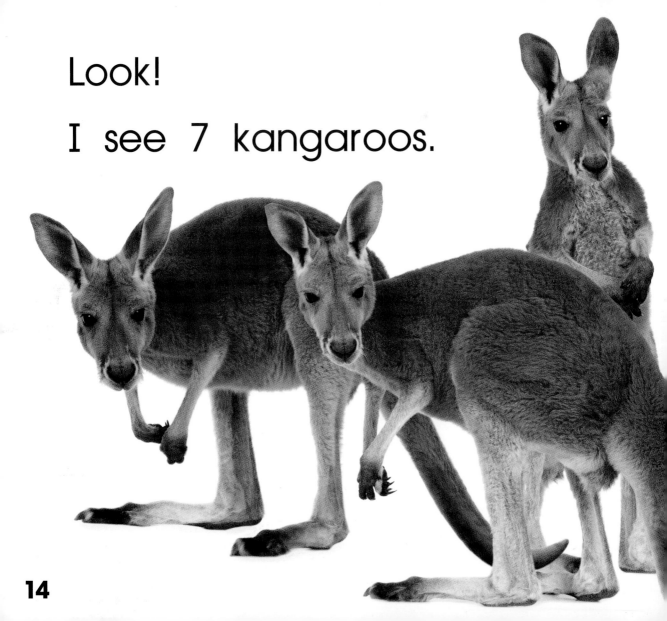

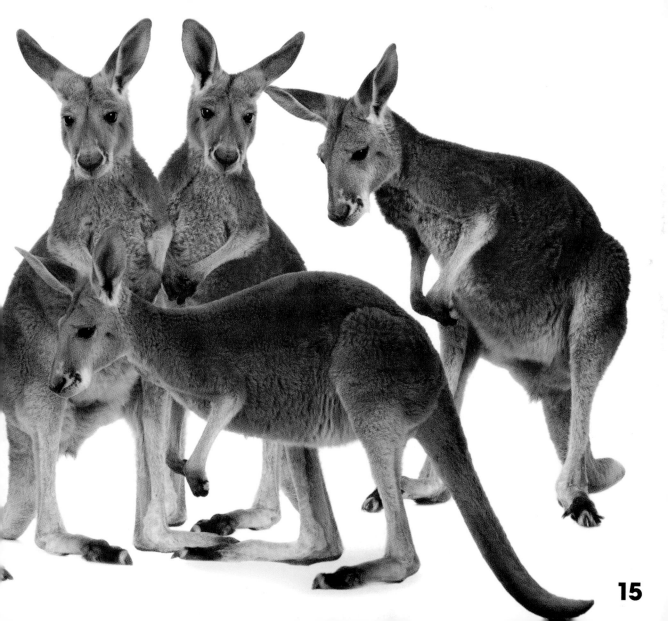

Look! I see animals.

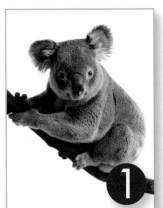

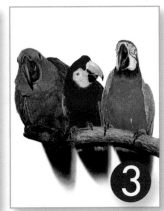

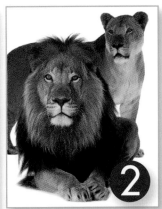

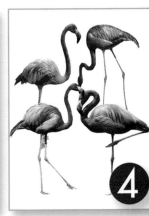

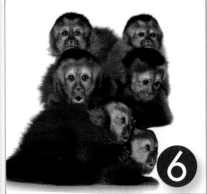

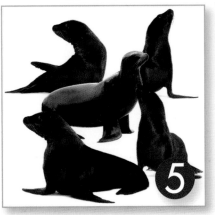

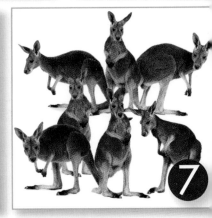